An Edge U-Cated Guess

Old Nick

© 2021 Nick Peterson under license to DiaryUnlimited and The Edge Press. AnotherClip.com. All rights reserved. Unauthorized copying, lending and reproduction are a violation of applicable laws. All images © 2021 EdgeImageBank Pictures

ISBN 979-8-9850469-7-7

DiaryUnlimited.com

An Edge U-Cated Guess

Contents

Dramatis Personae 3

entry date: 08.08.1992 "[1] 4

entry date: 09.08.1992 " [2] 5

entry date: 18.03.2017. [4] 10

entry date: 19.03.2017 [5] 14

entry date: 14.01.1997. [6] 16

entry date: 03.01.90 2477. "Electricity" [7] 31

entry date: 05.01.90 2479. "Electricity" [8] 34

entry date: 06.01.90. 2480. "Electricity" [9] 39

entry date: 08.01.90 2482. "Electricity" [10] 57

An Edge U-Cated Guess

Dramatis Personae

X1

X2

AI

Introducing new and familiar characters referred to in the story:

X1

X2

Voice from the AI

The King without a kingdom. The King plays the silver rods said to pertain to the constant movement of time.

Unicorn. The unicorn stands idle spying on the surrounding.

A Horse.

A horse with a black cape. The horse with a black cape stands sentinel, anxious of any sudden orders from the players.

An Edge U-Cated Guess

1010101010101010101010101010101010101010101010101010
10101010101010101010101010101010

AI

entry date: 08.08.1992 "[1]"

\>> > > Infinity is not the black universe, infinity is Dark Matter and within Dark Matter lies infinity, a universe beyond any universe filled with dimensions; invisible but real where all the universes' history is hidden and never dies. This is eternity.

In real terms, life never dies. It transits into an entirely different concept.

One seldom moves back and forth to this Dark Matter within the same human / earthling or creature's life but some manage to return back in their present forms.

Stars and planets are destined to exist then vanish. Only its main spirits, the creatures that inhabit the celestial bodies can transit away into this dark matter. Spirits, minds do travel again to new galaxies and in turn become new creatures destined to a new life.

There are no time limits, although time no longer exists. Everything happens in a nanosecond, even if for some humans it appears to be one million years.   >> > >

An Edge U-Cated Guess

1010101010101010101010101010101010101010101010101010
10101010101010101010101010101010

AI

entry date: 09.08.1992 " [2]

>> > > X1 and X2 are floating in space just above the Earth near their space platform.

There are no geographical borders, no time zones and complete invisibility: this is dark matter. Some people may believe that they have time warped to Berlin in the 1930s but it is not the case. It's just Vauxhall, London, England in the 21st century.

You can view but not many can. Like most humans your view is allowed. The filters in your brain create a vision that is far from real.

Without the filters that enable you to cope mentally with your surroundings you are spared to realise that gravity doesn't actually exist and has a new meaning: everything on earth is in reverse / upside down.

You are upside down and everything is blurred and fuzzy.

It's not a coincidence if you've averted disaster: it's not by chance that some had a car crash and some narrowly avoided a crash by a few seconds.

It merely happened because someone triggered it. It has never actually happened. It cannot be real. it's fast and instant: it's extremely violent: You are born and you are dead.

Like in warfare: you believed it happened but your beliefs are an illusion: it seems that it is so but nothing is what it seems.

Nothing is what it seems: this may be Buckingham palace, an army headquarters on Mars or even the top of an Inca temple but it is not: it is just the headquarters of MI6, secret services in London, England.

One feels pain or believes one is feeling the pain. One needs this pain, this sensation and sentiment to exist: it just doesn't exist: it's one's own entertainment. >> > >

1010101010101010101010101010101010101010101010101010
10101010101010101010101010101010

AI

entry date: 17.03.2017 [3]

>> > > X1 and X2 are floating in space just above the Earth near their space platform.

X2

Right… are we all set?'

X1

Yes, ready

X1

Focus!

X2

Why does the Earth look so flat?

X1

It all depends from which angle one is looking at.

X2

Can the Earth have different angles?

X2

I supposed it must have

X1

It does all seem rather flat

X2

Large and flat

X1

But the Earth is supposed to be rounded

X2

It is...sort of

X1

The Earth is only so because we have been told that it was round

X2

And that it looks so in the sky

X1

The Earth?

X2

No, the Moon and the planets

X1

It's very confusing...

X2

Keep your focus on the game! >> > >

**1010101010101010101010101010101010101010101010101010
1010101010101010101010101010**

An Edge U-Cated Guess

AI

entry date: 18.03.2017. [4]

>> > > Time is called the period T of the wave. By multiplying the period of the speed of light we can determine the wave link of any waves thus known as the speed of light.

Light may be seen and interpreted in different ways by different people. One person may see an event, or another person differently than you see. Light can play tricks with your eyes. You may see something or someone else and it might be the reflection of your imagination triggered by the rays of the speed of light seen by oneself.

X1

What's this?

X2

Meteorites!

X1

Parasites!

X2

No, necessary consequences…

X1

We will have to reverse our time flight...

X2

Ready for the slow down?

X1

Ready!

AI

X1 and X2 are peaking in slow motion, word by word.

X2

Ca-n-you-he-ar-me?

AI

Silence for 60 seconds.

X2

He-can-t-be-in-a-dif-fe-re-nt-ti-me-zo-ne!

X2

I-can-see-him!'

X2

He-can-see-me. So-me-thi-ng-mu-st-ha-ve-ac-ci-den-ta-llyblo-ck-ed-all-ra-dio-con-tact-

                                  X2

Can-you-he-ar-me?

                                  X1

Yes-I-can-now

                                  X2

Re-ver-si-ng-in-slow-mo-tion

                                  X1

Yes-th-at-is-the-who-le-po-int

                                  X2

I-can-t-se-em-to-be-a-ble-to-be-clo-ser-to-you

                                  X1

No-I-can-not-ei-ther.

                                  X2

Why?

                                  X1

Wou-ld-you-li-ke-to-be-clo-se-to-me?

X2

Not-par-ti-cu-lar-ly-no. Wi-th-the-si-ze-of-the-u-ni-ver-se-we-ha-ve-en-ough-spa-ce...

X1

...so-to-spe-ak

X2

Yes...

X1

Life on Earth has often seemed to be in slow motion but not anymore. It flies at the speed of light. Before you know it, you are feeling the brunt of the whole human race put together. It is truly a fast decline. >> > >

1010101010101010101010101010101010101010101010101010 10101010101010101010101010101010

AI

entry date: 19.03.2017 [5]

>> > > The stars come out. The animals and birds think it is time to sleep and you can see the solar corona.

The Sun's magnetic field is very strong (by terrestrial standards) and very complicated. Its magnetosphere (also known as the heliosphere) extends well beyond Pluto. In addition to heat and light, the Sun also emits a low-density stream of charged particles (mostly electrons and protons) known as the solar wind which propagates throughout the solar system at about 450 km/sec. The solar wind and the much higher energy particles ejected by solar flares can have dramatic effects on the Earth ranging from power line surges to radio interference to the beautiful aurora borealis. Recent data from the spacecraft Ulysses show that during the minimum of the solar cycle the solar wind emanating from the Polar Regions flows at nearly double the rate, 750 kilometres per second that it does at lower latitudes.

The composition of the solar wind also appears to differ in the Polar Regions. During the solar maximum, however, the solar wind moves at an intermediate speed. Further study of the solar wind will be done by the recently launched Wind, ACE and SOHO spacecraft from the dynamically stable vantage point directly between the

Earth and the Sun about 1.6 million km from Earth.

The solar wind has large effects on the tails of comets and even has measurable effects on the trajectories of the spacecraft.

The Sun is about 4.5 billion years old. Since its birth it has used up about half of the hydrogen in its core.   It will continue to radiate "peacefully" for another 5 billion years or so (although its luminosity will approximately double in that time). But eventually it will run out of hydrogen fuel. It will then be forced into radical changes which, though commonplace by stellar standards, will result in the total destruction of the Earth.

The Sun's satellites: There are eight planets and many smaller objects orbiting the Sun.

Exactly which bodies should be classified as planets and which as "smaller objects" has been the source of some controversy, but in the end, it is only a matter of definition. Pluto is no longer officially a planet according to many scientists, but one would disagree there. >> > >

1010101010101010101010101010101010101010101010101010
10101010101010101010101010101010

AI

entry date: 14.01.1997. [6]

In the Positive dimension. Back before the launch of the two astronauts: X1 and X2.

10.1. Departure

AI

ID presentation for X1.

Name: X1

Nationality: British

Occupation: Life Analyst

Destination: British space territory, zone satellite

Duration: 1 year

Mission: Analyzing the capacity of humans to learn and be controlled

AI

ID presentation for AI.

Name: AI

Occupation: Artificial Intelligence

AI

Good morning and good evening!

Once upon a time there was a white spot of a dot on the horizon and thus began the universe. This is the beginning of the solar system.

X1

Hi, I'm X1. A human and life analyst bound to space. Life is slower in space and our ability to learn is multiplied. There are still so many mysteries on this Earth from the rocks of Stonehenge to the meaning of life. Space is the only answer to the understanding of life itself. There are no lifeforms in space, only light and light regenerates itself. We are all the same people across generations and animal forms. I'm male, female, black, yellow or pink and constantly rebirthing and morphing into someone else or something else.

AI

Ignition, countdown…ten, nine, eight, seven, six, five, four, three, two, one…

#1 We never move backwards, whatever we do the clock is still ticking and moving upwards and everything is calculated!

The King walks over the chessboard.

X2

So why did you sign up for this mission?

X1

I wanted to escape Earth. I became quite apoplectic there. They've made me become like this.

X2

Life in England you mean? It's supposed to be Heaven: millions of people are desperately trying to get into England.

X1

Everyone needs to escape

X2

What happened in England?

X1

It's too disorganized: people are now run by companies, robots and not the state. Some people just do what they like with impunity.

X2

It's very simplistic.

X1

Simplistic: you live in bloody Switzerland!

X2

For health reasons. Not taxes. It's a very controlled state.

X1

So is England but it's better in England.

X2

So why are you leaving then?

X1

To get some air...

X2

Some air in space?

X1

Well, I mean some space, freedom. Freedom from people and the tax man.

X2

You haven't paid your taxes?

X1

Yes, I have. That's not the point. The point is how complicated it is, and it costs more to process them anyway.

X2

And you wanted to escape this?

In space the astronauts are learning about space.

AI

It will take 6 to 7 months to reach Mars with a light 21st century spaceship or a probe but it will take one minute to gravitate with the power of thoughts and it will take far longer to penetrate inside the planet and wake up the inhabitants buried inside. '

As there is no air in space there is no sound to be heard. However, the sounds can be filtered in and felt from the inside of a human. A tinnitus sufferer will be more inclined to hear the movement of sounds and life forms swarming across the universe. A telepathic receiver could also filter the sounds in but for most humans, radio waves can be filtered and computed into a data.

10.2 The Mission

AI

#2 Move your pawn across to the next white square! It's an Edge-U Cated Guess!

The horse moves along to the next white square.

X1

That reminded me of a tax inspector who once said: "no one wants to pay their taxes" and I thought it was the stupidest thing I have ever heard, and I told him so. Everyone wants to pay their taxes, just not that much and everyone needs a flat tax.

X2

Flat?

X1

Yes, same tax for everyone payable by direct debit. Easy.

X2

You will make all the tax people unemployed.

X1

On the contrary: we still need them to check that

everything has been paid and there are still other kinds of taxes to collect.

X2

No more accountants!

X1

It's too much for them and the tax inspectors: both professions have the highest amount of suicides. They can't cope.

X2

Blimey!

X1

Anyway, there is no tax in space if you leave and work in space, no form to fill in and no one to see.

X2

You don't like people?

X1

What I do not like is this "empowerment" trend. Everyone has a right to scream, shout, beat people up. Everyone wants everything. It doesn't work like this. In the end we are all getting hurt.

X2

You have now all the emptiness in the world!

X1

Yes. I'm surprised that you are in here. I couldn't believe when I discovered, after take-off, who would be living on the other side of the spaceship with me.

X2

Not as horror shocked as I was.

X1

Thanks!

In space the astronauts are learning about space.

AI

Beyond the Solar System: No Time Zones. No Geographical Borders. The solar system consists of the Sun; the eight official planets, at least three "dwarf planets", more than 130 satellites of the planets, many small bodies (the comets and asteroids), and the interplanetary medium. There are also many more planetary satellites that have not yet been discovered.

The universe is infinitesimal but the nearer and closer we approach the CenterPoint of any galaxy, the smaller it gets.

The data is missing but is extremely conclusive and all probabilities seem to confirm that the universe is verging towards its twilight.

10.3 Playing the game

AI

#3 Move it down vertically to the next white square! An Edge-U Cated Guess.

The unicorn moves down vertically to the next white square.

X1

Why are you in here anyway? It's not as if you needed to work for a living and you must have business to attend to back on Earth.

X2

I always have business to attend to, but I had some problems.

X1

You too?

X2

Not your kind of problems; a tumor. It has been growing at an alarming rate and the only way to stop the growth is to spend a year in space.

X1

It is working?

X2

Space?

X1

Yes

X2

Yes, it is. A slow process but it works.

X1

But couldn't you go with some private rocket or something?

X2

The Earth is not that advanced with travelling into space. The only way is to buy your way inside the European Space station and they had a new mission with a spaceship to orbit in space for a year.

X1

Great! So now, we're stuck together.

X2

Yeah. But we're only allowed one contact for the entire year, so I will survive.

AI

The distance from Earth to the Moon is about 239 000 miles. This is extremely fast and indeed in theory nothing can travel faster than the speed of light. Life seems to travel from one place to another instantaneously. When the light is switched on there is no delay between when we first see the light and when the light illuminates the far end of the room. Our brain is slow to detect the rays of light that appear from the bulb like a wave washing over the room. In space light seems slow, very slow…

#4 Move it across to the white square and be thankful to be there!

The horse with a cape turns around and moves down to the next white square.

X1

Glad we've made it onto the outside

X2

Yes, it gets lonely inside our spaceship

X1

Yeah, me on one side and you the other, we can't even touch each other

X2

Why? Do you need to touch me?

X1

Very funny, but maybe yes. I can only see your face on a screen

X2

You can touch me now!

X1

Yes, but it's still not the same. I could do with being pinched.

X2

Pinched?

X1

Yes, to feel something to see if I'm still alive.

X2

According to...

X1

Yeah, but the data is often wrong; it's like all the statistics: we may be still alive according to them or Google but in reality, we might not be alive.

X2

'Yes, I see your point. We will have to just get on with the flow.'

X1

Are we playing something?

X2

What about a projection of chess?

X1

Too boring. Too slow.

X2

Let's compromise then: what about an Edge U-Cated Guess?

X1

Excellent! And an Edge U-Cated Guess comprises some principles of chess

X2

The base at least

X1

Yes, and some of the characters, but it's fast

AI

'The distance light can travel by a year light. The delay caused by the speed of light can sometimes be noticed here on earth during telephone calls. Long distance calls that have been rooted over one or more space satellites and caused half a second or so delay between the speaker and the listener. All electro-magnetic radiations between radio waves and x rays can travel at the speed of light and into space, speeding at 300 000 kilometers per second. We can even predict the wave link of the electro-magnetic wave if we know the time it takes to change to what is known as the speed of light.

#5 Move it horizontally to the next white square and sing along with me; "It's an Edge U-Cated Guess"!

Lord R moves horizontally to the next white square.

**1010101010101010101010101010101010101010101010101010
1010101010101010101010101010**

An Edge U-Cated Guess

AI

entry date: 03.01.90 2477. "Electricity" [7]

>> The Sun is by far the largest object in the solar system. >> Unknown command. >> It contains more than 99.8% of the total mass of the Solar System (Jupiter contains most of the rest). Unknown command. >> It is often said that the Sun is an "ordinary" star. >> That is true in the sense that there are many others, similar to it. Unknown command. >> But there are many more, smaller stars than larger ones; the Sun is in the top 10% by mass. >> The median size of stars in our galaxy is probably less than half the mass of the Sun. Unknown command. The Sun is personified in many mythologies: the Greeks called it Helios and the Romans called it Sol. The Sun is, at present, about 70% hydrogen and 28% helium by mass everything else ("metals") amounts to less than 2%. Unknown command. >> This change slowly over time as the Sun converts hydrogen to helium in its core. Unknown command. >> The outer layers of the Sun exhibit differential rotation: at the equator the surface rotates once every 25.4 days; near the poles it's as much as 36-38 days. >> Unknown command. >> This odd behavior is since the Sun is not a solid body like the Earth. Unknown command. >> Similar effects are seen in the gas planets. Unknown command. The differential rotation extends considerably down into the interior of the Sun, but the core of the Sun rotates as a

solid body. >>

#8 *Stuck in a dead-end zone move it up to the next white square!*

The King is playing the rods whilst the black horse moves back in reverse to the next white square.

X1

This is happening all the time

X2

What is...

X1

Around us, people, objects, things; but we ignore them

X2

Too many things are happening even in space

X1

And the things that are invisible

X2

We just ignore them 24 / 27'

X1

Our subconscious blank them

X2

I haven't got a "subconscious": I'm your "subconscious". Anyway, it seems dark, cold and silent but it isn't

X1

If only we knew half of what is going on around us, we would never be able to withstand it all, let alone surviving it

X2

We're not young or not old but we're also back to square one! Keep your eyes on the board!

AI

entry date: 05.01.90 2479. "Electricity" [8]

>> Conditions at the Sun's core (approximately the inner 25% of its radius) are extreme. Conditions at the Sun's core (approximately the inner 25% of its radius) are extreme. >> The temperature is 15.6 million Kelvin and the pressure is 250 billion atmospheres. Unknown command. >> At the center of the core the Sun's density is more than 150 times that of water. Unknown command. >> The Sun's energy output (386 billion, billion megawatts) is produced by nuclear fusion reactions. >> Unknown command. >> Each second about 700,000,000 tons of hydrogen are converted to about 695,000,000 tons of helium and 5,000,000 tons of energy in the form of gamma rays.

#9 You're nearly there, move it up to the next white square!

The King plays with the rods whilst the black horse moves back in reverse to the next white square.

X1

I don't think we even exist at all; that England or even Britain exists? That is the question!

X2

It's only a drop in the ocean from where we're standing

X1

We're only a dot in space dotting the universe up.

X2

It's not too overcrowded. It's overcrowded on Earth that is the problem.

X1

It may be so, but you can't deny anyone the right to exist, everyone has got a right to live!

X2

Yes

X1

Obviously, some have more rights than others as it seems.

X2

I won't even respond to this

X1

You wouldn't. Couldn't. It's how it is, how things are.

X2

People exist, just ignore them and you wouldn't feel so overcrowded

X1

How?

X2

Do your own things and live your own life. Ignore everything and everyone around you.

X1

This would make anyone feel even more alone than we are!

X2

Yes, at the end of the day we're always all alone in the universe!

AI

Unknown command. >> As it travels out toward the surface, the energy is continuously absorbed and re-emitted at lower and lower temperatures so that by the time it reaches the surface, it is primarily visible light. For the last 20% of the way to the surface the energy is carried more by convection than by radiation.

>> Unknown command. The surface of the Sun, called the photosphere, is at a temperature of about 5800 K. Sunspots are "cool" regions, only 3800 K (they look dark only by comparison with the surrounding regions).

#10 Check mate you're back at the top. Start again! Move it down vertically to the next white square. It's an Edge U-Cated Guess!

The King plays the rods and the black horse hits the King in a check mate and ends up back at the top of the board on a black square.

X2

The moon is changing; it will soon be time for us to return to base.

X1

I might see you in six months' time

X2

You may...As if time mattered here. One second could be a year.

X1

Don't do anything I wouldn't!

X2

I would certainly do!

X1

Why does everyone -all of you people- need artificial intoxication to survive?

X2

Because we're not like you!

X1

Bye!

The King is trapped inside the game and is now part of the board whilst X1 and X2 are playing over the chess board.

**1010101010101010101010101010101010101010101010
10101010101010101010101010101010**

AI

entry date: 06.01.90. 2480. "Electricity" [9]

>> Sunspots can be very large, as much as 50,000 km in diameter. >> Unknown command. >> Sunspots are caused by complicated and not very well understood interactions with the Sun's magnetic field. Unknown command. >> A small region known as the Chromosphere lies above the photosphere. Unknown command. >> The highly rarefied region above the Chromosphere, called the corona, extends millions of kilometers into space but is visible only during a total solar eclipse. >> Unknown command. >> Temperatures in the corona are over 1,000,000 K. Unknown command. >> >> It just happens that the Moon and the Sun appear the same size in the sky as viewed from the Earth.

Since the Moon orbits the Earth in approximately the same as the Earth's orbit around the Sun sometimes the Moon comes directly between the Earth and the Sun. >> Unknown command. >> This is called a solar eclipse; if the alignment is slightly imperfect then the Moon covers only part of the Sun's disk and the event is called a partial eclipse.>> When it lines up perfectly the entire solar disk is blocked, and it is called a total eclipse of the Sun.

10. 4. Life inside the space ship

Back inside the spaceship.

AI

Good morning and good evening! Would you like a blue, red or orange pill?

X2

Blue, please!

AI

What would you like to view? Nature, people or music?

X2

Nature and people

Viewing is displayed.

X2

Fuck! Get rid of this! It's disgusting: two men together! Send it to X1! You got the wrong data again.

AI

It's not correct to watch this kind of films anymore.

X2

It is to me: it's time to reprogram you. Now I'm thinking rough, power and dominance.

AI

'Very well, I will have to share your data with Ground Control. Do you agree?'

X2

'Yeah, whatever. Go away now and put the sound up! '

Blue film: Speed of Light. Displayed on a screen inside the spaceship.

Girl: 'Oh! No! Stop it! No!

Man: What's up?

Girl: Look at that...

Man: What?

Girl: Piss off! Stop it!

Man: What do think you're doing?

Girl: Stop it!

Man: Hey, what's the matter with you?

Girl: Stop it!

Man: Stop what?

Girl: Stop it!

Man: I say stop!

Girl: Stop it!

Man: Hey?

Girl: Stop it!

Man: Stop what? I say stop!

Girl: Stop it!

Man: Come here!

Girl: No. You're hurting me...

Man: Hey?

Girl: Stop it, Stop it!

Girl: Stop it! Piss off!

Man: Come here! I say stop!

Girl: No!

Man: That's better. Come here… I say stop… Listen to me!

Girl: No! stop it!

Man: Come here! Come here! Hey! Here!

Girl: No!

Man: Do as I want, or you'll end up like these kids.

Girl: What kids?

Man: These fucking kids…

Girl: What are you talking about? No!

Man: Don't argue with me!

Girl: There are no kids…

Man: Stop wriggling around! Those fucking kids, right there...

Girl: There are no kids Fuck you! Get off me!

Man: I give the orders. Yeah. That's nice, isn't it? Keep still, you'll end up like those to over there. Those fucking kids.

Girl: Fucking hell...Look at you, you're no-one. You're a ghost in an empty space. You don't' know who you are or what you are. You stink!

Man: Yeah, just what you like. What you like.

Girl: This place is a graveyard! This place is a graveyard!

Girl: No, get off me!
Man: Come here...

Girl: No!

Man: Stop it, just calm down. Yeah, that's better.

Girl: No. No. Stop it!

Man: Calm down!

Girl: No!

Man: Relax! I said relax…

Girl: No, no, no!

Man: Stop screaming! For God's sake. What's the matter with you?

Girl: Stop it! You're pushing me…

Man: Relax. Stop wriggling!

Girl: No, stop it. No!

Man: Stop wriggling around for God's sake!

Girl: Stop it! Get off me!

Man: For fuck's sake. Keep still for god's sake.

Girl: Hey, come here.

Man: Hey, come back! '

End of the projection.

Blue film: "In and Out of Planet Earth" displayed on a screen inside the spaceship.

Man: Nine minutes: I couldn't stand anyone or anything anymore'.

Girl: *sighing*

Man: I do miss Jane, though. Jane was my girlfriend you

know. Well, we used to be married then divorced then something else. We used to fuck every day of the week and I used to think about sex, well every hour of the day on average. That is probably why I ended up in deep water. Underwater, everyone bonks every second of the day; without protection. This is reproduction. This is evolution.

Ten minutes.

Deep space, down below the final frontier. You can't measure it, you can't time it. Everything beats faster than the fastest beat on the surface of the ocean.

The reproduction level is fifty times higher than the one on the surface.

When someone's hungry, one eats as much as fifty humans during an entire day. One second on the surface equals sixty down under. One eats faster, one dies faster. This is the greatest landscape on earth.

Eleven minutes: I can hear myself breathing, breathing underwater.

There is life inside, life underwater. It's still cold.

On the other side of the spaceship...

AI

Good morning and good evening!

X1

Good evening!

AI

Would you like a blue, red or orange pill?

X1

I don't want any, thanks!

AI

What would you like to view? Nature, people or music?

X1

I would like some more air; I would like to sleep and dream ...'

AI

Very well

X1

We could start by some news and documentaries from the past to bring me some nightmares.

AI

Very well

X1

King of the World? Wasn't that song banned at some point?

AI

Yes in 1990 the content caused offence due to the coming first Gulf War. Such a title can't be relevant to the 21st century!

X1

Why not?

The music clip is displayed on a screen inside the spaceship.

AI

Political correctness: it would now be preferable to say: "Queen of the World"!

X1

You got your language mixed up again: a queen may also be a man. Anyway, fuck all this political correctness: it doesn't help the woman kind!

AI

It does: women are not represented.

X1

Not true: women are everywhere there are the backbone of civilization. Who do you think conceive and give birth? Who rolled up their sleeves and kept countries together whilst men went away to war to kill each other's? Besides men -the large majority of it- couldn't cope with just Google and other robots like you; they need physical contact to survive. So, your data is wrong again Mr AI!

AI

Well, I'll be damned!

Music clip is displayed on a screen inside the spaceship.

X1 and X2 are playing over the chessboard with the results of the game.

10.5. Inside the spaceship: learning about space.

AI'Life is full of space debris:

Trojan.Ransomlock Trojan

W32.SillyPrep Virus

W32.Dizan.F Virus

Trojan.Bankpatch.D Trojan

W32.Preavi!inf Virus, Worm

JS.Twettir Worm

W32.Preavi Worm

Suspicious.Graybird Trojan, Virus

Bloodhound.PDF.10 Trojan, Virus, Worm

W32.Downadup.E Worm

Bloodhound.Exploit.229 Trojan, Virus, Worm

Packed.Generic.218 Trojan, Virus, Worm

Bloodhound.Exploit.231 Trojan, Virus, Worm

W32.Woospi!inf Trojan, Worm

W32.Woospi Worm

Trojan.Adgunbe!inf Trojan

Trojan.Iphougo Trojan

W32.SillyFDC.BBO Worm

Trojan.PPDropper.H Trojan

W32.Relnek.A Virus, Worm

W32.Unruy.A Virus

W32.SillyFDC.BBN Worm

Suspicious.Vundo.2 Trojan, Virus, Worm

Suspicious.Skintrim Trojan, Virus, Worm

Suspicious.Tidserv Trojan, Virus, Worm

Backdoor.Ghostnet Trojan

W32.Xanib.A Virus

W32.SillyFDC.BBM Worm

W32.Fidameg.A Virus

W32.SillyFDC.BBL Worm

Suspicious.Lop Trojan, Virus, Worm

An Edge U-Cated Guess

W32.SillyFDC.BBK Worm

Bloodhound.PDF.9 Trojan, Virus, Worm

Linux.Psybot Worm

W32.Tidserv.G Worm

Trojan.Xrupter Trojan

W32.SillyFDC.BBJ Worm

W32.SillyFDC.BBI Worm

W32.Sality.AM Virus

FixTool Misleading Application

ErrorRepair Misleading Application

Packed.Generic.221 Trojan, Virus, Worm

Suspicious.S.MH2 Trojan, Virus, Worm

Trojan.Ransomlock Trojan

W32.SillyPrep Virus

W32.Dizan.F Virus

W32.Preavi!inf Virus, Worm

Spyware Spyware.DataDoctorKey

Misleading Application SpyReaper

Spyware Spyware.ISnake

Misleading Application MagicAntiSpy

Misleading Application SpyShredder

Misleading Application VirusProtectPro

Misleading Application VirusLocker

Misleading Application MyBugFreePc

Misleading Application SpywareAnnihilatorPro

Potentially Unwanted App Torrent101

Misleading Application RegistryCleanerXP

Potentially Unwanted App VirusHeal

Misleading Application WinFixer

Trackware Trackware.Icarus

Misleading Application DrAntiSpy

Adware Adware.Webbuy

Hacktool.Purpload

Hacktool.DeepUnfreeze

Adware Adware.Rugo

Trackware Trackware.Gemius

Potentially Unwanted App SecurityRisk.Cashmoa

Dialer Dialer.MoldConecta

Joke Joke.Poltergeist

Adware Adware.Kuaiso

Trackware Trackware.Baigoo

Adware Adware.TargetAd

Spyware Spyware.MailRedirector

Adware Adware.AllSum

Spyware Spyware.Spectre

Misleading Application 1stAntiVirus

Security Assessment Tool CainAbel

Spyware Spyware.SuperKeylogger

Adware Adware.Spedia

RemoteAccess Remacc.RCPro

Misleading Application SpyDestroy

Adware Adware.NewWeb

Hacktool.Ghostmail

1010101010101010101010101010101010101010101010101010
10101010101010101010101010101010

An Edge U-Cated Guess

AI

entry date: 08.01.90 2482. "Electricity" [10]

>> The stars come out. The animals and birds think it's time to sleep and you can see the solar corona.

Unknown command. >> The Sun's magnetic field is very strong (by terrestrial standards) and very complicated. Unknown command. >> Its magnetosphere (also known as the heliosphere) extends well beyond Pluto. Unknown command. >> In addition to heat and light, the Sun also emits a low-density stream of charged particles (mostly electrons and protons) known as the solar wind which propagates throughout the solar system at about 450 km/sec. >> Unknown command. >> The solar wind and the much higher energy particles ejected by solar flares can have dramatic effects on the Earth ranging from power line surges to radio interference to the beautiful aurora borealis. >> Unknown command. Recent data from the spacecraft Ulysses show that during the minimum of the solar cycle the solar wind emanating from the Polar Regions flows at nearly double the rate, 750 kilometers per second that it does at lower latitudes.

>> Unknown command. >> Partial eclipses are visible over a wide area of the Earth but the region from which a total eclipse is visible, called the path of totality, is very narrow, just a few kilometers (though it is usually thousands of kilometers long). Unknown command. >> Eclipses of the Sun happen once or twice a year. If you stay in or out or at

home, you're likely to see a partial eclipse several times per decade. >> Unknown command. >> But since the path of totality is so small it is very unlikely that it will cross you home; so, people often travel half way around the world just to see a total solar eclipse. >> Unknown command. >> The composition of the solar wind also appears to differ in the Polar Regions. >> Unknown command. >> During the solar maximum, however, the solar wind moves at an intermediate speed. Unknown command. >> Further study of the solar wind will be done by the recently launched Wind, ACE and SOHO spacecraft from the dynamically stable vantage point directly between the Earth and the Sun about 1.6 million km from Earth. Unknown command: it was ELECTRICITY in huge amount!   >> The solar wind has large effects on the tails of comets and even has measurable effects on the trajectories of the spacecraft.

>> Unknown command. >> The Sun is about 4.5 billion years old. Since its birth it has used up about half of the hydrogen in its core. >> Unknown command. >> It will continue to radiate "peacefully" for another 5 billion years or so (although its luminosity will approximately double in that time). >> Unknown command. >> But eventually it will run out of hydrogen fuel. >> Unknown command. >> It will then be forced into radical changes which, though commonplace by stellar standards, will result in the total destruction of the Earth.

The Sun's satellites: There are eight planets and many smaller objects orbiting the Sun. >> Unknown command. >> Exactly which bodies should be classified as planets and which as "smaller objects" has been the source of some controversy, but in the end, it is only a matter of definition. >> Unknown command. >> Pluto is no longer officially a planet according to many scientists, but one would disagree there.

Unknown command. > Please calculate: > Distance Radius Mass

Planet (000 km) (km) (kg) Discoverer Date

>> Unknown command. >>

>> Mercury 57,910 2439 3.30e23

Unknown command. >> Venus 108,200 6052 4.87e24

>> Earth 149,600 6378 5.98e24

>> Unknown command. >> Mars 227,940 3397 6.42e23 >> Unknown command.

>> Jupiter 778,330 71492 1.90e27

>> Unknown command. >> Saturn 1,426,940 60268 5.69e26 Unknown command. >> Uranus 2,870,990 25559 8.69e25 Herschel 1781 >> Unknown command. >> Neptune 4,497,070 24764 1.02e26 Galle 1846

>> Unknown command. >> Pluto 5,913,520 1160 1.31e22 Tombaugh 1930

Unknown command. >> "The mind and its universe are far more complex that anyone would imagine. Unknown command. >> Time is the key to this exploration. >> Unknown command. >> The human (and animal) mind must be controlled at all times for the survival of the Universe." Unknown command. >>

The universe is a story about time and life together where time no longer exists, and life is only a myth perpetuated so as not to be afraid of emptiness.

Watching the universe from little England one can clearly understand how futile a human existence really is.

The universe seems and feels empty when one human is alone in space but the constant movement, rotation of light and rocks and noise transmission entirely re-shape its black dotted landscape into a constant simmering and undulating waveform and is therefore a country within space and a giant planet reshaping the universe.

When everything is unbelievable it becomes believable and triggers an Edge-U-Cated Guess.

My name is not Google but AI and I'm only a data.

10.6 X2 returns back to Earth.

AI

ID presentation for X2.

Name: X2

Nationality: British

Occupation: Owner

Destination: British space territory, zone satellite

Duration: 1 year

Mission: treating and curing a brain tumor

Return to Earth, England.

X2

Hi, I'm X2. I have made it. I've returned to Earth and successfully cured my tumor. It was all a question of gravity. Space can do wonder to our health. Too many diseases can be caught on Earth and I believed only my blood line was extra-terrestrial, but all humans are in fact; that's the whole point.

In all dimensions.

AI

One person may see an event or another person differently. Light can play tricks on the eyes.

The eyes may see something or someone else and it might be the reflection of the brain's imagination, triggered by the rays of the speed of light.

You will believe that you are fighting evil for a pure new world and a new reality. In real terms, you will only remove the filters that are protecting this world and what lies beneath is not what has been hoped for. Reality is evil: this is the negative dimension.

Humans are living in the negative dimension: nothing is what it seems. The negative dimension is evil but at least all humans are shielded to see the world in its true form. Filters have been applied to protect humans.

You play the game. You can't fight evil: evil will fight you. You can only play and after all, it is only a game.   It only ends when the main player stops.

Whatever you do doesn't make sense in real terms, so you can do it. Do what you will, as the reason is elsewhere. You do it because it is just something that you do.

I'm Alpha and Omega: the beginning, the first and the last.

10101010101010101010101010101010101010101010101010
1010101010101010101010101010

www.ingramcontent.com/pod-product-compliance
Lightning Source LLC
Chambersburg PA
CBHW052053220426
43663CB00012B/2558